Piano Solos

ANDREW LLOYD WEBBER
F O R   P I A N O

T0048371

CONTENTS

ISBN 978-0-7935-1503-5

HAL•LEONARD®
CORPORATION

7777 W. BLUEMOUND RD. P.O. BOX 13819 MILWAUKEE, WI 53213

ALL I ASK OF YOU

(From "THE PHANTOM OF THE OPERA")

Music by ANDREW LLOYD WEBBER
Lyrics by CHARLES HART
Additional lyrics by RICHARD STILGOE

mp   molto rit.

p

8va

ANY DREAM WILL DO

(From "JOSEPH AND THE AMAZING TECHNICOLOR DREAMCOAT")

Words by TIM RICE
Music by ANDREW LLOYD WEBBER

Add pedal

THE LAST MAN IN MY LIFE

(From "SONG & DANCE")

Music by ANDREW LLOYD WEBBER
Lyrics by DON BLACK

DON'T CRY FOR ME ARGENTINA

(From The Opera "EVITA")

Lyrics by TIM RICE
Music by ANDREW LLOYD WEBBER

MCA music publishing

I DON'T KNOW HOW TO LOVE HIM

(From "JESUS CHRIST SUPERSTAR")

Lyrics by TIM RICE
Music by ANDREW LLOYD WEBBER

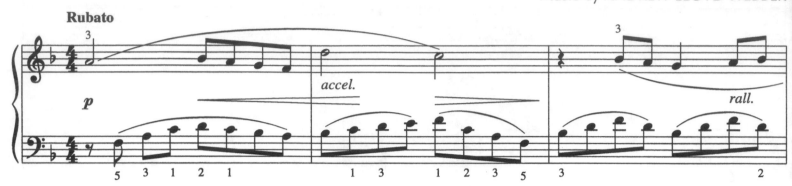

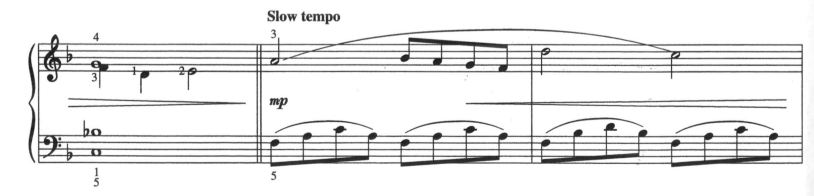

MCA music publishing

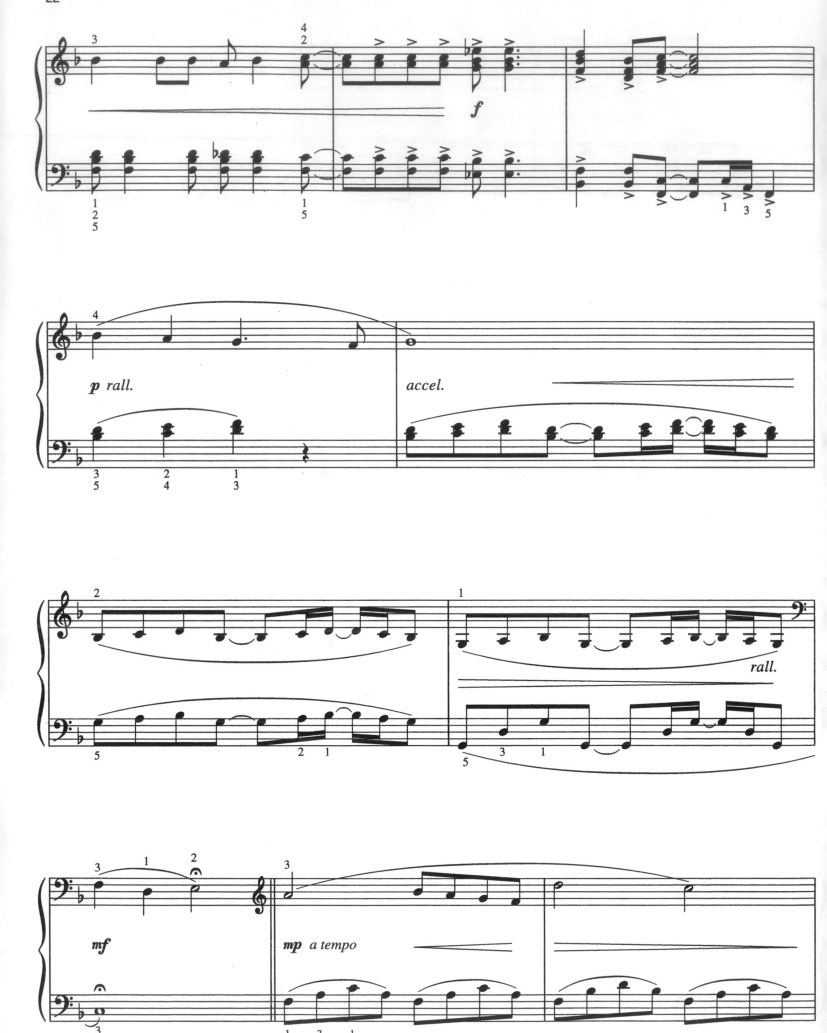

JESUS CHRIST SUPERSTAR

(From "JESUS CHRIST SUPERSTAR")

Words by TIM RICE
Music by ANDREW LLOYD WEBBER

MCA music publishing

No pedal

Repeat and Fade

LOVE CHANGES EVERYTHING

(From "ASPECTS OF LOVE")

Music by ANDREW LLOYD WEBBER
Lyrics by DON BLACK and CHARLES HART

Moderately

MEMORY

(From "CATS")

Music by ANDREW LLOYD WEBBER
Text by TREVOR NUNN after T.S. ELIOT

THE MUSIC OF THE NIGHT
(From "THE PHANTOM OF THE OPERA")

Music by ANDREW LLOYD WEBBER
Lyrics by CHARLES HART
Additional lyrics by RICHARD STILGOE

PIE JESU
(From "REQUIEM")

Music by ANDREW LLOYD WEBBER

Religioso, not too fast

ONLY YOU
(From "STARLIGHT EXPRESS")

Words by RICHARD STILGOE
Music by ANDREW LLOYD WEBBER

THE PHANTOM OF THE OPERA

(From "THE PHANTOM OF THE OPERA")

Music by ANDREW LLOYD WEBBER
Lyrics by CHARLES HART
Additional lyrics by RICHARD STILGOE
and MIKE BATT

WISHING YOU WERE SOMEHOW HERE AGAIN

(From "THE PHANTOM OF THE OPERA")

Music by ANDREW LLOYD WEBBER
Lyrics by CHARLES HART
Additional lyrics by RICHARD STILGOE

UNEXPECTED SONG
(From "SONG & DANCE")

Music by ANDREW LLOYD WEBBER
Lyrics by DON BLACK

A bit faster